Can You Drink the Cup?

Henri J.M. Nouwen

foreword by
RON HANSEN

ave maria press AmP notre dame, indiana

Founded in 1865, Ave Maria Press is a ministry of the Indiana Province of Holy Cross.

www.avemariapress.com

ISBN-10 1-59471-099-6   ISBN-13 978-1-59471-099-5

Cover photo © photos.com

Our thanks to Henri's brother, Laurent, for the lovely photo of Henri's chalice.

Cover and text design by David R. Scholtes

Printed and bound in the United States of America.

"When the late Cardinal Joseph Bernardin learned that his cancer had returned and that he hadn't long to live, he turned immediately to Henri Nouwen for spiritual support. This little book explains why. In concise and elegant language, *Can You Drink the Cup?* opens up Nouwen's own life in Christ and enlarges ours. I loved the book—and needed it."

Kenneth L. Woodward
Contributing Editor, *Newsweek*

"Can You Drink the Cup? weaves personal encounter, profound compassion for the Other, and the vibrant reality of God's Word into a brilliant whole. It is, quite simply, a classic."

Lawrence S. Cunningham
John A. O'Brien Professor of Theology,
The University of Notre Dame

OTHER BOOKS BY
HENRI J.M. NOUWEN
published by Ave Maria Press

Behold the Beauty of the Lord

Heart Speaks to Heart

In Memoriam

Out of Solitude

With Open Hands

Eternal Seasons
edited by Michael Andrew Ford

The Dance of Life
edited by Michael Andrew Ford

Learn more about Nouwen, his writing, and the work of the
Henri Nouwen Society at www.HenriNouwen.org.

In Memory of

Adam John Arnett
November 17, 1961–February 13, 1996

Contents

Acknowledgments

This little book was written during the first few months of my sabbatical year, a year that the l'Arche Daybreak community gave me for my writing. I am deeply grateful to all the members of the community, and especially to Nathan Ball, the director, and Sue Mosteller, the pastor, for their encouragement and support during this time away from home.

I also owe much gratitude to Peggy McDonnell, her family and friends who, in memory of Murray McDonnell, offered me the financial support for my writing.

I wrote *Can You Drink the Cup?* while staying with Hans and Margaret Kruitwagen in Oakville, Ontario, and with Robert Jonas, Margaret Bullitt-Jonas, and their son, Sam, in Watertown, Massachusetts. Their great kindness and generous hospitality offered me the ideal context for reflection and writing. A special word of thanks goes to Margaret Bullitt-Jonas's mother, Sarah Doering, who offered me the use of her third-floor apartment while she made a three-month Buddhist retreat.

I am also most grateful to Kathy Christie for her very competent and efficient secretarial help and for her great patience with my many "urgent" calls and "important" changes of mind. Her friendship is a real gift to me. A special word of thanks goes to Susan Brown, whose last minute line-editing was an unexpected blessing, and to Wendy Greer, who made many valuable corrections.

Finally, I want to thank my editor Frank Cunningham at Ave Maria Press for his long-term interest in my writing and his special care for the presentation of this text.

I dedicate *Can You Drink the Cup?* to Adam Arnett, my friend and teacher about whom I wrote in these pages. Adam died on February 13, 1996, just at the time this text was finished. I hope and pray that his life and death will continue to bear much fruit in the lives of all those who have known him and loved him so much.

by Ron Hansen

The symbols of blood and wine were connected in biblical times. The Jews recognized blood as a life force, created injunctions against consuming it, shed it as a sin offering, feared being defiled by it, and recalled it as a sign of the covenant with God in their annual celebration of deliverance at Passover. Wine was called the "blood of grapes" (Genesis 49:11) and became a sign of friendship and accord, a gift of rejuvenation that was festive, luxurious, and a harbinger of the heavenly banquet, yet if overindulged in could lead to drunkenness and sin.

Jesus united these symbols at the Lord's Supper when he took the cup of red wine, offered thanks for it, and gave it to the apostles while saying, "This cup is the new covenant in my blood, which will be shed for you."

In sharing the wine, those loyal to Christ were joining him in an offering of their own blood for the sake of others. Christ's new covenant was not like that made with their forefathers and inscribed on the stone tablets of Moses, but was the covenant announced by Jeremiah, in which the Lord declared: "I will put my teaching into their inmost being and inscribe it upon their hearts. Then I will be their God, and they shall be my people. . . . I will forgive their iniquities, and remember their sins no more" (Jeremiah 31:33, 34).

The blessing cup of wine became Christ's blood, a source of life and salvation for those who shared it. But Christ, of course, had to undergo death by crucifixion so that others could be "justified by his blood" (Romans 5:9). In the scene that provides the basis for this inspiring book's title (Matthew 20:20–23), Jesus cautions Zebedee's sons about the cup—the calling, and association—they have chosen in him, implying that it's paradoxical, a yes and a no: a cup of wine but also of blood, of freedom but obedience, of happiness and peace in spite of consternation or persecution, of the guarantee of eternal life but only after the usual human lot of anguish, illness, and death.

In Luke's gospel, there is a sequence of actions in the Lord's Supper: Jesus takes the cup, gives thanks, then shares the cup with his disciples. In Henri Nouwen's introduction to the spiritual life, he meditates on holding, lifting, and drinking that cup.

Holding the cup of life is, for Nouwen, a way of looking critically at who we really are, accepting our various skills, inadequacies, and differences from others, and rejoicing in our radical singularity.

Lifting the cup "is an invitation to affirm and celebrate life together." It means joining in community and sharing our cravings, our fantasies, our shame, our vulnerabilities, and giving others permission to do likewise in a spirit of blessing, of giving thanks.

Nouwen writes that, "Drinking the cup of life is fully appropriating and internalizing our own unique existence, with all its sorrows and joys." It is the challenge to forthrightly acknowledge who we are, to forsake the entrapments of our addictions, compulsions, and sins, and to be as fully trusting in God as Jesus was when he, in a spirit of unconditional love, accepted his ministry with all its consequences.

Written while Nouwen was pastor of the L'Arche Daybreak community of men and women with intellectual disabilities and their assistants, *Can You Drink the Cup?* invokes a number of stories of people whose simplicity and honesty have informed his thinking and inspired his love. L'Arche Daybreak's stated mission is:

"To create homes where faithful relationships based on forgiveness and celebration are nurtured.

"To reveal the unique value and vocation of each person.

"To change society by choosing to live relationships in community as a sign of hope and love."

Can You Drink the Cup? presents holding, lifting, and drinking the cup of life as ways of fulfilling those lofty goals.

Then the mother of Zebedee's sons came with her sons to make a request of Jesus, and bowed low; and he said to her, "What is it that you want?" She said to him, "Promise that these two sons of mine may sit one at your right hand and the other at your left in your kingdom." Jesus answered, "You do not know what you are asking. Can you drink the cup that I am going to drink?" They replied, "We can." He said to them, "Very well; you shall drink my cup, but as for seats at my right hand and my left, these are not mine to grant; they belong to those to whom they have been allotted by my Father."

Matthew 20:20–23

The Chalice and the Cup

It was Sunday, July 21, 1957. Bernard Alfrink, the Cardinal Archbishop of the Netherlands, laid his hands on my head, dressed me with a white chasuble, and offered me his golden chalice to touch with my hands bound together with a linen cloth. Thus, along with twenty-seven other candidates, I was ordained to the priesthood in St. Catherine's Cathedral in Utrecht. I will never forget the deep emotions that stirred my heart at that moment.

Since I was six years old, I had felt a great desire to be a priest. Except for a few fleeting thoughts of becoming a navy captain, mostly because of the influence of the men with their blue and white uniforms and golden stripes parading the railroad platform of our town, I always dreamt about one day being able to say Mass, as my uncle Anton did.

My maternal grandmother was my great supporter. An astute businesswoman, she had built a large department store, where my mother did some part-time bookkeeping work and where I could run around, use the elevators freely, and play hide-and-seek with my younger brother. As soon as she discovered my budding vocation to the priesthood, she ordered her store carpenter to build me a child-size altar and had her seamstress sew all the vestments necessary to play priest. By the time I was eight years old, I had converted the attic of our home to a children's chapel, where I played Mass, gave sermons to my parents and relatives, and set up a whole hierarchy with bishops, priests, deacons, and altar servers among my friends. Meanwhile, my grandmother not only continued to give me new things to play priest with, such as chalices and plates, but also gently introduced me to a life of prayer and encouraged me in a personal relationship with Jesus.

When I was twelve years old I wanted to go to the minor seminary, but both my parents felt that I was much too young to leave home. "You are not ready to make a decision about the priest-hood," my father told me. "You better wait until you are eighteen." It was 1944, and they wanted me to go to a gymnasium in our town, close to Amsterdam. The Second World War had come to a very critical stage, but my parents were able to keep me and my brother away from the cruel-ties of war and even provided us with a rather regular school life. After the war we moved to The Hague, where I finished my secondary edu-cation. Finally, in 1950, I went to the seminary to study philosophy and theology and prepare myself for ordination.

On that 21st day of July, 1957, when my life-long dream to become a priest was realized, I was a very naive twenty-five-year-old. My life had been well-protected. I had grown up as in a beautifully kept garden surrounded by thick hedges. It was a garden of loving parental care, innocent boy scout experiences, daily mass and communion, long hours of study with very pa-tient teachers, and many years of happy but very isolated seminary life. I came out of it all full of love for Jesus, and full of desire to bring the Gospel to the world, but without being fully aware that not everybody was waiting for me. I had only met—and that quite cautiously—a few Protestants, had never encountered an unbeliever, and certainly had no idea about other religions. Divorced people were unknown to me, and if there were any priests who had left the priesthood, they were kept away from me. The greatest "scandal" I had experienced was a friend leaving the seminary!

Still, life in the garden of my youth was quite beautiful and offered me invaluable gifts for the rest of my life: a joyful spirit, a deep devotion for Jesus and Mary, a true desire to pray, a great love for theology and spirituality, a good knowledge of contemporary languages, a serious interest in scripture and the early Christian writers, an enthusiasm about preaching, and a very strong sense of vocation. My maternal grandmother, my paternal grandparents, my parents, friends, and teachers all encouraged me to trust my desire to live a life with Jesus for others.

When Cardinal Alfrink handed me the chalice, I felt ready to start a life as a priest. The joy of that day still lives in me as a precious memory. The chalice was the sign of that joy.

Most of my classmates had chalices made for their ordination. I was an exception. My uncle Anton, who was ordained in 1922, offered

This chalice was Anton's gift for Nouwen's ordination.

me his chalice as a sign of his gratitude that a new priest had come into our family. It was beautiful, made by a famous Dutch goldsmith and adorned with my grandmother's diamonds. The foot was decorated with a crucifix shaped as a tree of life, from which golden grapes and grape leaves grew to cover the node and bowl. Around the rim of the foot these Latin words were engraved: "*Ego sum vites, vos palmites*," which means, "I am the vine, you are the branches." It was a very precious gift, and I was deeply moved to receive it. I remember saying to my uncle: "I have seen you celebrating Mass so often with this chalice; can you really do without it?" He smiled and said, "I want you to have it. It comes from your grandmother, who died too soon to see you as a priest but whose love for you, her oldest grandchild, is with you today." When I still hesitated to accept the chalice, he said: "Take it, but pass it on to the next member of our family who will be ordained."

The chalice is still with me, because so far no one else in my family has been ordained to the priesthood. I keep it in the sacristy of the Dayspring Chapel in Toronto, where I now live. I often show it to friends and visitors. But so much has happened during the thirty-seven years that followed my ordination that my uncle's decorated golden chalice no longer expresses what I am presently living. During the Eucharist today, I use several large cups made by the glassblower Simon Pearce in Vermont. The precious golden chalice that could only be touched and used by an ordained priest is replaced by large glass cups in which the wine can be seen and from which many can drink. These glass cups speak about a new way of being a priest and a new way of being human. I am happy with these cups on the altar table today, but without the golden chalice given me by my uncle Anton nearly forty years ago, they would not mean as much to me as they do.

The Question

In this book I want to tell the story of the cup, not just as my story, but as the story of life.

When Jesus asks his friends James and John, the sons of Zebedee, "Can you drink the cup that I am going to drink?" he poses the question that goes right to the heart of my priesthood and my life as a human being. Years ago, when I held that beautiful golden chalice in my hands, that question didn't seem hard to answer. For me, a newly ordained priest full of ideas and ideals, life seemed to be rich with promises. I was eager to drink the cup!

Today, sitting in front of a low table surrounded by men and women with mental disabilities and their assistants, and offering them the glass cups of wine, that same question has become a spiritual challenge. Can I, can we, drink the cup that Jesus drank?

I still remember the day, a few years ago, when the story in which Jesus raises that question was read during the Eucharist. It was 8:30 in the morning, and about twenty members of the Daybreak community were gathered in the little basement chapel. Suddenly the words "Can you drink the cup?" pierced my heart like the sharp spear of a hunter. I knew at that moment—as with a flash of insight—that taking this question seriously would radically change our lives. It is the question that has the power to crack open a hardened heart and lay bare the tendons of the spiritual life.

"Can you drink the cup? Can you empty it to the dregs? Can you taste all the sorrows and joys? Can you live your life to the full whatever it will bring?" I realized these were our questions.

But why should we drink this cup? There is so much pain, so much anguish, so much violence. Why should we drink the cup? Wouldn't it be a lot easier to live normal lives with a minimum of pain and a maximum of pleasure?

After the reading, I spontaneously grabbed one of the large glass cups standing on the table in front of me and looking at those around me— some of whom could hardly walk, speak, hear, or see—I said: "Can we hold the cup of life in our hands? Can we lift it up for others to see, and can we drink it to the full?" Drinking the cup is much more than gulping down whatever happens to be in there, just as breaking the bread is much more than tearing a loaf apart. Drinking the cup of life involves *holding*, *lifting*, and *drinking*. It is the full celebration of being human.

Can we hold our life, lift our life, and drink it, as Jesus did? In some of those around me, there was a sign of recognition, but in myself there was a deep awareness of truth. Jesus' question had given me a new language with which to speak about my life and the lives of those around me. For a long time after that simple morning Eucharist, I kept hearing Jesus' question: "Can you drink the cup that I am going to drink?" Just letting that question sink in made me feel very uncomfortable. But I knew that I had to start living with it.

This book is the fruit of having done that. It strives to make Jesus' question pierce our hearts so that a personal answer can emerge from there. I will follow the three themes that emerged that morning in the Dayspring Chapel: *holding, lifting,* and *drinking.* They will allow me to explore the spiritual horizons that Jesus' question opens for us and to invite you who will read this to join me in this exploration.

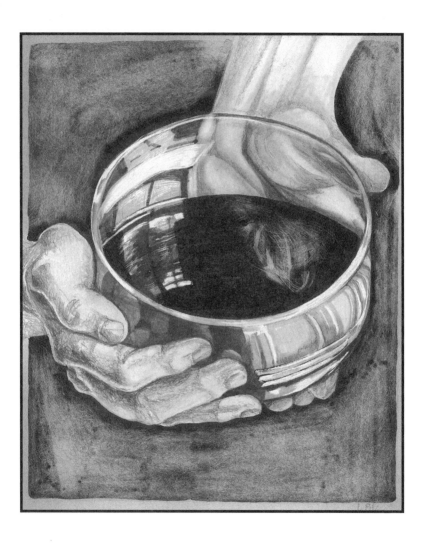

PART ONE

Holding the Cup

CHAPTER ONE

Holding

---

*Before we drink the cup,
we must hold it!*

I still remember a family dinner long ago in the Netherlands. It was a special occasion, but I have forgotten whether it was a birthday, a wedding, or an anniversary. Since I was still a young boy, I was not allowed to drink wine, but I was fascinated by the way the grown-ups were drinking their wine! After the wine had been poured into the glasses, my uncle took his glass, put both of his hands around the cup, moved the glass gently while letting the aroma enter his nostrils, looked at all the people around the table, lifted it up, took a little sip, and said: "Very good . . . a very good wine . . . let me see the bottle . . . it must be a fiftier."

This was my uncle Anton, my mother's oldest brother, priest, monsignor, authority in many things, good wines being one of them. Every time uncle Anton came to family dinners, he had a comment or two to make about the wine that was served. He would say, "A full body," or "Not what I expected," or "Could be a little hardier," or "This is just good with the roast," or "Well, for fish this is okay." His criticisms were not always appreciated by my father, who provided the wine, but nobody dared to contradict him. The whole ritual around the wine intrigued me as a child. Often my brothers and I would tease our uncle, saying: "Well, uncle Anton, can you guess the year this wine was made without looking at the label? You are the expert, aren't you?"

One thing I learned from it all: drinking wine is more than just drinking. You have to know what you are drinking, and you have to be able to talk about it. Similarly, just living life is not enough. We must know what we are living. A life that is not reflected upon isn't worth living. It belongs to the essence of being human that we contemplate our life, think about it, discuss it, evaluate it, and form opinions about it. Half of living is reflecting on what is being lived.

Is it worth it? Is it good? Is it bad? Is it old? Is it new? What is it all about? The greatest joy as well as the greatest pain of living come not only from what we live but even more from how we think and feel about what we are living. Poverty and wealth, success and failure, beauty and ugliness aren't just the facts of life. They are realities that are lived very differently by different people, depending on the way they are placed in the larger scheme of things. A poor person who has compared his poverty with the wealth of his neighbor and thought about the discrepancy lives his poverty very differently than the person who has no wealthy neighbor and has never been able to make a comparison. Reflection is essential for growth, development, and change. It is the unique power of the human person.

Holding the cup of life means looking critically at what we are living. This requires great courage, because when we start looking, we might be terrified by what we see. Questions may arise that we don't know how to answer. Doubts may come up about things we thought we were sure about. Fear may emerge from unexpected places. We are tempted to say: "Let's just live life. All this thinking about it only makes things harder." Still, we intuitively know that without looking at life critically we lose our vision and our direction. When we drink the cup without holding it first, we may simply get drunk and wander around aimlessly.

Holding the cup of life is a hard discipline. We are thirsty people who like to start drinking at once. But we need to restrain our impulse to drink, put both of our hands around the cup, and ask ourselves, "What am I given to drink? What is in my cup? Is it safe to drink? Is it good for me? Will it bring me health?"

Just as there are countless varieties of wine, there are countless varieties of lives. No two lives are the same. We often compare our lives with those of others, trying to decide whether we are better or worse off, but such comparisons do not help us much. We have to live our life, not someone else's. We have to hold *our own* cup. We have to dare to say: "This is my life, the life that is given to me, and it is this life that I have to live, as well as I can. My life is unique. Nobody else will ever live it. I have my own history, my own family, my own body, my own character, my own friends, my own way of thinking, speaking, and acting—yes, I have my own life to live. No one else has the same challenge. I am alone, because I am unique. Many people can help me to live my life, but after all is said and done, I have to make my own choices about how to live."

It is hard to say this to ourselves, because doing so confronts us with our radical aloneness. But it is also a wonderful challenge, because it acknowledges our radical uniqueness.

I am reminded of Philip Sears's powerful sculpture of Pumunangwet, the Native American at the Fruitlands Museums in Harvard, Massachusetts. He stands with his beautifully stretched naked body, girded with a loincloth, reaching to the heavens with his bow high above him in his left hand while his right hand still holds the memory of the arrow that just left for the stars. He is totally self-possessed, solidly rooted on the earth, and totally free to aim far beyond himself. He knows who he is. He is proud to be a lonesome warrior called to fulfill a sacred task. He truly holds his own.

Like that warrior we must hold our cup and fully claim who we are and what we are called to live. Then we too can shoot for the stars!

CHAPTER TWO

The Cup of Sorrow

When I first came to l'Arche Daybreak, I saw much sorrow.

I was asked to care for Adam, a twenty-two-year-old man who could not speak, could not walk alone, did not show signs of recognition. He had a curved back, suffered from daily epileptic seizures, and often had intestinal pains. When I first met Adam, I was afraid of him. His many handicaps made him a stranger to me, a man I wanted to avoid.

Soon after I met Adam I also came to know his brother Michael. Although Michael could speak a little and was able to walk by himself and even fulfill some minor tasks, he too was severely handicapped and needed constant attention to make it through the day. Adam and Michael are the only children of Jeanne and Rex.

Michael lived at home until he was twenty-five and Adam until he was eighteen. Jeanne and Rex would have loved to continue to keep the boys at home. However, time was eroding the physical resources required to look after their sons and so they entrusted them to the l'Arche Daybreak community, hoping to find a good home for them there.

I was quite overwhelmed with the sorrows of this little family. Four people burdened by worries and pain, by fear of unexpected complications, by the inability to communicate clearly, by a sense of great responsibility, and by an awareness that life will only become harder as age increases.

But Adam, Michael, and their parents are part of a much greater sorrow. There is Bill, who suffers from muscular dystrophy, who needs a pacemaker for his heart and a breathing machine for his lungs during the night, and who is in constant fear of falling. He has no parents to visit. His parents never were able to care for him, and both died at a rather young age.

There is Tracy, completely paralyzed, but with a bright mind, always struggling to find ways to express her feelings and thoughts. There is Susanne, not only mentally disabled but also regularly battered by inner voices that she cannot control. There is Loretta, whose disability causes her to feel unwanted by family and friends and whose search for affection and affirmation throws her into moments of deep despair and depression. There are David, Francis, Patrick, Janice, Carol, Gordie, George, Patsy . . . each of them with a cup full of sorrow.

Surrounding them are men and women of different ages, from different countries and religions, trying to assist these wounded people. But they soon discover that those they care for reveal to them their own less visible but no less real sorrows: sorrows about broken families, sexual unfulfillment, spiritual alienation, career doubts, and most of all, confusing relationships. The more they look at their own often wounded pasts and confront their uncertain futures, the more they see how much sorrow there is in their lives.

And for me things are not very different. After ten years of living with people with mental disabilities and their assistants, I have become deeply aware of my own sorrow-filled heart. There was a time when I said: "Next year I will finally have it together," or "When I grow more mature these moments of inner darkness will go," or "Age will diminish my emotional needs." But now I know that my sorrows are mine and will not leave me. In fact I know they are very old and very deep sorrows, and that no amount of positive thinking or optimism will make them less. The adolescent struggle to find someone to love me is still there; unfulfilled needs for affirmation as a young adult remain alive in me. The deaths of my mother and many family members and friends during my later years cause me continual grief. Beyond all that, I experience deep sorrow that I have not become who I wanted to be, and that the God to whom I have prayed so much has not given me what I have most desired.

But what is our sorrow in a little community in Canada, compared with the sorrow of the city, the country, and the world? What about the sorrow of the homeless people asking for money on the streets of Toronto, what about the young men and women dying of AIDS, what about the thousands who live in prisons, mental hospitals, and nursing homes? What about the broken families, the unemployed, and the countless disabled men and women who have no safe place such as Daybreak?

And when I look beyond the boundaries of my own city and country, the picture of sorrow becomes even more frightening. I see parentless children roaming the streets of São Paulo like packs of wolves. I see young boys and girls being sold as prostitutes in Bangkok. I see the emaciated prisoners of war in the camps of former Yugoslavia. I see the naked bodies of people in Ethiopia and Somalia wandering aimlessly in the eroded desert. I see millions of lonely, starving faces all over the world, and large piles of the dead bodies of people killed in cruel wars and ethnic conflicts. Whose cup is this? It is our cup, the cup of human suffering. For each of us our sorrows are deeply personal. For all of us our sorrows, too, are universal.

Now I look at the man of sorrows. He hangs on a cross with outstretched arms. It is Jesus, condemned by Pontius Pilate, crucified by Roman soldiers, and ridiculed by Jews and Gentiles alike. But it is also us, the whole human race, people of all times and all places, uprooted from the earth as a spectacle of agony for the entire universe to watch. "When I am lifted up from the earth," Jesus said, "I shall draw all people to myself" (John 12:32). Jesus, the man of sorrows, and we, the people of sorrow, hang there between heaven and earth, crying out, "God, our God, why have you forsaken us?"

"Can you drink the cup that I am going to drink?" Jesus asked his friends. They answered yes, but had no idea what he was talking about. Jesus' cup is the cup of sorrow, not just his own sorrow but the sorrow of the whole human race. It is a cup full of physical, mental, and spiritual anguish. It is the cup of starvation, torture, loneliness, rejection, abandonment, and immense anguish. It is the cup full of bitterness. Who wants to drink it? It is the cup that Isaiah calls "the cup of God's wrath. The chalice, the stupefying cup, you have drained to the dregs," (Isaiah 51:17) and what the second angel in the Book of Revelation calls "the wine of retribution" (Revelation 14:8), which Babylon gave the whole world to drink.

When the moment to drink that cup came for Jesus, he said: "My soul is sorrowful to the point of death" (Matthew 26:38). His agony was so intense that "his sweat fell to the ground like great drops of blood" (Luke 22:44). His close friends James and John, whom he had asked if they could drink the cup that he was going to drink, were there with him but fast asleep, unable to stay awake with him in his sorrow. In his immense loneliness, he fell on his face and cried out: "My Father, if it is possible, let this cup pass me by" (Matthew 26:39). Jesus couldn't face it. Too much pain to hold, too much suffering to embrace, too much agony to live through. He didn't feel he could drink that cup filled to the brim with sorrows.

Why then could he still say yes? I can't fully answer that question, except to say that beyond all the abandonment experienced in body and mind Jesus still had a spiritual bond with the one he called Abba. He possessed a trust beyond betrayal, a surrender beyond despair, a love beyond all fears. This intimacy beyond all human intimacies made it possible for Jesus to allow the request to let the cup pass him by become a prayer directed to the one who had called him "My Beloved." Notwithstanding his anguish, that bond of love had not been broken. It couldn't be felt in the body, nor thought through in the mind. But it was there, beyond all feelings and thoughts, and it maintained the communion underneath all disruptions. It was that spiritual sinew, that intimate communion with his Father, that made him hold on to the cup and pray: "My Father, let it be as you, not I, would have it" (Matthew 26:39).

Jesus didn't throw the cup away in despair. No, he kept it in his hands, willing to drink it to the dregs. This was not a show of willpower, staunch determination, or great heroism. This was a deep spiritual yes to Abba, the lover of his wounded heart.

When I contemplate my own sorrow-filled heart, when I think of my little community of people with mental handicaps and their assistants, when I see the poor of Toronto, and the immense anguish of men, women, and children far and wide on our planet, then I wonder where the great yes has to come from. In my own heart and the hearts of my fellow people, I hear the loud cry "O God, if it is possible, let this cup of sorrow pass us by." I hear it in the voice of the young man with AIDS begging for food on Yonge Street, in the little cries of starving children, in the screams of tortured prisoners, in the angry shouts of those who protest against nuclear proliferation and the destruction of the planet's ecological balance, and in the endless pleas for justice and peace all over the world. It is a prayer rising up to God not as incense but as a wild flame.

From where then will come that great yes? "Let it be as you, not I, will have it." Who can say yes when the voice of love hasn't been heard! Who can say yes when there is no Abba to speak to? Who can say yes when there is no moment of consolation?

In the midst of Jesus' anguished prayer asking his Father to take his cup of sorrow away, there was one moment of consolation. Only the Evangelist Luke mentions it. He says: "Then an angel appeared to him, coming from heaven to give him strength" (Luke 22:43).

In the midst of the sorrows is consolation, in the midst of the darkness is light, in the midst of the despair is hope, in the midst of Babylon is a glimpse of Jerusalem, and in the midst of the army of demons is the consoling angel. The cup of sorrow, inconceivable as it seems, is also the cup of joy. Only when we discover this in our own life can we consider drinking it.

CHAPTER THREE

The Cup of Joy

After my nine years at the Daybreak community, Adam, Michael, Bill, Tracy, Susanne, Loretta, David, Francis, Patrick, Janice, Carol, Gordie, George, and many others who live at the heart of our community have become my friends. More than friends, they are an intimate part of my daily life. Although they still are as handicapped as when I first met them, I seldom think of them as people with handicaps. I think of them as brothers and sisters with whom I share my life. I laugh with them, cry with them, eat dinners with them, go to the movies with them, pray and celebrate with them—in short, live my life with them. They truly fill me with immense joy.

After caring for Adam for a few months, I was no longer afraid of him. Waking him up in the morning, giving him a bath and brushing his teeth, shaving his beard and feeding him breakfast had created such a bond between us—a bond beyond words and visible signs of recognition—that I started to miss him when we couldn't be together. My time with him had become a time of prayer, silence, and quiet intimacy. Adam had become a true peacemaker for me, a man who loved and trusted me even when I made the water for his bath too hot or too cold, cut him with the razor, or gave him the wrong type of clothes to wear.

His epileptic seizures no longer scared me either. They simply caused me to slow down, forget about other obligations, and stay with him, covering him with heavy blankets to keep him warm. His difficult and very slow walk no longer irritated me but gave me an opportunity to stand behind him, put my arms around his waist, and speak encouraging words as he took one careful step after the other. His spilling a glass full of orange juice or dropping his spoon with food on the floor no longer made me panic but simply made me clean up. Knowing Adam became a privilege for me. Who can be as close to another human being as I could be to Adam?

Who can spend a few hours each day with a man who gives you all his confidence and trust? Isn't that what joy is?

And Michael, Adam's brother: what a gift his friendship became! He became the only one in the community who calls me "Father Henri." Every time he says that, there is a smile on his face, suggesting that he really should be a Father too! With his halting, stuttering voice, he keeps saying, pointing to the large stole around my neck, "I . . . want . . . that . . . too . . . Father." When Michael is sad because his brother is sick, or because he has many seizures himself, or because someone he loves is leaving, he comes to me, puts his arms around me, and lets his tears flow freely. Then after a while he grabs me by the shoulder, looks at me, and with a big smile breaking through his tears he says: "You are . . . a . . . funny . . . Father!" When we pray together, he often points to his heart and says: "I feel . . . it . . . here . . . here in my heart." But as we hold hands, there is that immense joy that emerges from our shared sorrow.

Bill, the man with so many setbacks in his life, has become my special companion. He often comes with me on speaking trips. We have gone to Washington, New York, Los Angeles, and many other places over the years, and wherever we go, Bill's cheerful presence is as important as my many words. Bill loves to tell jokes. In his simple, direct, unself-conscious way, he entertains people for hours, whether they are wealthy or poor, dignitaries or simple folks, bishops or table servers, members of parliament or elevator operators. For Bill, everyone is important and everyone deserves to hear his jokes. But at moments Bill's sorrows can become too much for him. Sometimes when he talks about Adam, who cannot talk, or Tracy, who cannot walk, he bursts into tears. Then he puts his arms on my shoulders and cries openly, without embarrassment. And after a while his smile returns and he continues his story.

Then there is Tracy's radiant smile when a friend comes to see her, Loretta's gentle care for those who are much more handicapped than she, and the many little ways in which David, Janice,

Carol, Gordie, George, and the others pay attention to each other and to their assistants. They all are true signs of joy.

It is not surprising that many young men and women from all over the world want to come to Daybreak to be close to these special people. Yes, they *come* to care for them and help them in their needs. But they *stay* because those they came to care for have brought them a joy and peace they had not been able to find anywhere else. Sure, the handicapped members of Daybreak put them in touch with their own handicaps, their own inner wounds and sorrows, but the joy that comes from living together in a fellowship of the weak makes the sorrow not just tolerable but a source of gratitude.

My own life in this community has been immensely joyful, even though I had never suffered so much, cried so much, and anguished so much as at Daybreak. Nowhere am I as well known as in this little community. It is totally impossible to hide my impatience, my anger, my frustration, and my depression from people who are so in touch with their own weakness. My needs for friendship, affection, and affirmation are right there for everyone to see. I have never experienced so deeply that the true nature of priesthood is a compassionate-being-with. Jesus' priesthood is described in the letter to the Hebrews as one of solidarity with human suffering. Calling myself a priest today radically challenges me to let go of every distance, every little pedestal, every ivory tower, and just to connect my own vulnerability with the vulnerability of those I live with. And what a joy that is! The joy of belonging, of being part of, of not being different.

Somehow my life at Daybreak has given me eyes to discover joy where many others see only sorrow. Talking with a homeless man on a Toronto street doesn't feel so frightening anymore. Soon money is not the main issue. It becomes: "Where are you from? Who are your friends? What is happening in your life?" Eyes meet, hands touch, and there is—yes, often completely unexpected—a smile, a burst of laughter, and a true moment of joy. The sorrow is still there, but something has changed by my no longer standing in front of others but sitting with them and sharing a moment of togetherness.

And the immense suffering of the world? How can there be joy among the dying, the hungry, the prostitutes, the refugees, and the prisoners? How does anyone dare to speak about joy in the face of the unspeakable human sorrows surrounding us?

And yet, it is there! For anyone who has the courage to enter our human sorrows deeply, there is a revelation of joy, hidden like a precious stone in the wall of a dark cave. I got a glimpse of that while living with a very poor family in Pamplona Alta, one of the "young towns" at the outskirts of Lima, Peru. The poverty there was greater than any I had seen before, but when I think back on my three months with Pablo, Maria, and their children, my memories are filled with laughter, smiles, hugs, simple games, and long evenings just sitting around telling stories. Joy, real joy was there, not a joy based on success, progress, or the solution of their poverty, but bursting forth from the resilient human spirit, fully alive in the midst of all odds. And when

Heather, the daughter of New York friends, recently returned from ten months' relief work in Rwanda, she had seen more than despair. She had also seen hope, courage, love, trust, and true care. Her heart was deeply troubled, but not crushed. She has been able to continue her life in the United States with a greater commitment to work for peace and justice. The joys of living were stronger than the sorrows of death.

The cup of life is the cup of joy as much as it is the cup of sorrow. It is the cup in which sorrows and joys, sadness and gladness, mourning and dancing are never separated. If joys could not be where sorrows are, the cup of life would never be drinkable. That is why we have to hold the cup in our hands and look carefully to see the joys hidden in our sorrows.

Can we look up to Jesus as to the man of joys? It seems impossible to see joy in the tortured, naked body hanging with outstretched arms on a wooden cross. Still, the cross of Jesus is often presented as a glorious throne on which the King is seated. There the body of Jesus is portrayed not as racked by flagellation and crucifixion but as a beautiful, luminous body with sacred wounds.

The cross of San Damiano that spoke to St. Francis of Assisi is a good example. It shows the crucified Jesus as a victorious Jesus. The cross is surrounded by splendid gold; the body of Jesus is a perfect, immaculate human body; the horizontal beam on which he hangs is painted as the open grave from which Jesus rose; and all those gathered under the cross with Mary and John are full of joy. At the top we can see God's hand, surrounded by angels, drawing Jesus back into heaven.

This is a resurrection cross, in which we see Jesus lifted up in glory. Jesus' words "When I am lifted up from the earth, I shall draw all people to myself," (John 12:32) refer not only to his crucifixion but also to his resurrection. Being lifted up means not only being lifted up as the crucified one but also being lifted up as the risen one. It speaks not only about agony but also about ecstasy, not only about sorrow but also about joy.

Jesus makes this very clear when he says: "As Moses lifted up the snake in the desert, so must the Son of man be lifted up so that everyone who believes may have eternal life in him" (John 3:14–15). What Moses raised in the desert as a standard was a bronze serpent, healing everyone bitten by snakes who looked up at it (Numbers 21:8–9). The cross of Jesus is likewise the standard of healing, not just healing from physical wounds, but healing from the human condition of mortality. The risen Lord draws all people with him into his new and eternal life. Jesus who cries out, "My God, my God, why have you forsaken me?" (Matthew 27:47) also says in total surrender: "Father, into your hands I commit my spirit" (Luke 23:46). Jesus, who participated fully in all our pain, wants us to participate fully in his joy. Jesus the man of joy wants us to be the people of joy.

"Can you drink the cup that I am going to drink?" When Jesus brought this question to John and James, and when they impulsively answered with a big "We can," he made this terrifying, yet hope-filled prediction: "Very well; you shall drink my cup." The cup of Jesus would be their cup. What Jesus would live, they would live. Jesus didn't want his friends to suffer, but he knew that for them, as for him, suffering was the only and necessary way to glory. Later he would say to two of his disciples: "Was it not necessary that the Christ should suffer before entering into his glory?" (Luke 24:26). The "cup of sorrows" and the "cup of joys" cannot be separated. Jesus knew this, even though in the midst of his anguish in the garden, when his soul was "sorrowful to the point of death" (Matthew 26:38), he needed an angel from heaven to remind him of it. Our cup is often so full of pain that joy seems completely unreachable. When we are crushed like grapes, we cannot think of the wine we will become. The sorrow overwhelms us, makes us throw ourselves on the ground, face down, and sweat drops of blood. Then we need to be reminded that our cup of sorrow is also our cup of joy and that one day we will be able to taste the joy as fully as we now taste the sorrow.

Soon after the angel had given him strength, Jesus stood up and faced Judas and the cohort who had come to arrest him. When Peter drew his sword and struck the high priest's servant,

Jesus said to him, "Put your sword back in its scabbard; am I not to drink the cup that the Father has given me?" (John 18:11).

Now Jesus is no longer overcome by anguish. He stands in front of his enemies with great dignity and inner freedom. He holds his cup filled with sorrow but with joy too. It is the joy of knowing that what he is about to undergo is the will of his Father and will lead him to the fulfillment of his mission. The Evangelist John shows us the enormous power that emanates from Jesus. He writes: "Knowing everything that was to happen to him, Jesus came forward and said [to Judas and the cohort], 'Who are you looking for?' They answered, 'Jesus the Nazarene.' He said, 'I am he.' . . . When Jesus said to them, 'I am he,' they moved back and fell on the ground" (John 18:5–6).

Jesus' unconditional yes to his Father had empowered him to drink his cup not in passive resignation but with the full knowledge that the hour of his death would also be the hour of his glory. His yes made his surrender a creative act, an act that could bear much fruit. His yes took away the fatality of the interruption of his ministry. Instead of a final irrevocable end, his death became the beginning of a new life. Indeed, his yes enabled him to trust fully in the rich harvest the dying grain would yield.

Joys are hidden in sorrows! I know this from my own times of depression. I know it from living with people with mental handicaps. I know it from looking into the eyes of patients, and from being with the poorest of the poor. We keep forgetting this truth and become overwhelmed by our own darkness. We easily lose sight of our joys and speak of our sorrows as the only reality there is.

We need to remind each other that the cup of sorrow is also the cup of joy, that precisely what causes us sadness can become the fertile ground for gladness. Indeed, we need to be angels for each other, to give each other strength and consolation. Because only when we fully realize that the cup of life is not only a cup of sorrow but also a cup of joy will we be able to drink it.

PART TWO

Lifting the Cup

CHAPTER FOUR

Lifting

Good manners were very important in our family, especially table manners.

In the hall of our home hung a large bell. Ten minutes before dinner, my father rang the bell loudly and announced: "Dinnertime, everybody wash their hands."

There were many "table sins": elbows on the table, heaping up food on your spoon or fork, eating fast, making noises, chewing with your mouth open, not using your fork and knife while eating meat, using your knife to cut spaghetti. Many of our meals were interspersed with my father's little commands: "Elbows off the table," "Wait until everyone is served," and "Don't talk as you eat."

As I became older, I was allowed to have a glass of wine. It was a sign of adulthood. In 1950, when I was eighteen years old, drinking wine was a luxury. In France and Italy, wine at dinner was part of daily life, but in Holland it was a sign of a festive occasion. When we had wine there were special rituals: tasting and approving the wine, saying a few good words about it, pouring it into the glasses—only half full—and, most important of all, lifting it for a toast.

No one in our family would ever drink from his or her glass before everyone had been served and my father had lifted up his glass, looked at each of us, spoken a word of welcome, and emphasized the uniqueness of the occasion. Then, with his glass he touched my mother's glass and the glasses of his guests and drank a little. It always was a solemn and important moment, a moment with a sacred quality. In later years, when wine was no longer so special, when glasses were filled to the brim, and when people drank without lifting their glasses or offering a toast, I always felt that something was missing, yes, even that something was lost.

Lifting up the cup is an invitation to affirm and celebrate life together. As we lift up the cup of life and look each other in the eye, we say: "Let's not be anxious or afraid. Let's hold our cup together and greet each other. Let us not hesitate to acknowledge the reality of our lives and encourage each other to be grateful for the gifts we have received."

We say to each other: in Latin, "*Prosit*" (be well); in German, "*Zum Wohl*" (to your well-being); in Dutch, "*Op je gezondheid*" (to your health); in English, "*Cheers*"; in French, "*A votre santé*" (to your health); in Italian, "*Alla tua salute*" (to your health); in Polish, "*Sto lat*" (a hundred years); in Ukrainian, "*Na zdorvia*" (to your health); in Hebrew, "*L'chaim*" (to life).

The best summary of all these wishes is, "to life." We lift the cup to life, to affirm our life together and celebrate it as a gift from God. When each of us can hold firm our own cup, with its many sorrows and joys, claiming it as our unique life, then too, can we lift it up for others to see and encourage them to lift up their lives as well. Thus, as we lift up our cup in a fearless gesture, proclaiming that we will support each other in our common journey, we create community.

Nothing is sweet or easy about community. Community is a fellowship of people who do not hide their joys and sorrows but make them visible to each other in a gesture of hope. In community we say: "Life is full of gains and losses, joys and sorrows, ups and downs—but we do not have to live it alone. We want to drink our cup together and thus celebrate the truth that the wounds of our individual lives, which seem intolerable when lived alone, become sources of healing when we live them as part of a fellowship of mutual care."

Community is like a large mosaic. Each little piece seems so insignificant. One piece is bright red, another cold blue or dull green, another warm purple, another sharp yellow, another shining gold. Some look precious, others ordinary. Some look valuable, others worthless. Some look gaudy, others delicate. As individual stones, we can do little with them except compare them and judge their beauty and value. When, however, all these little stones are brought together in one big mosaic portraying the face of Christ, who would ever question the importance of any one of them? If one of them, even the least spectacular one, is missing, the face is incomplete. Together in the one mosaic, each little stone is indispensable and makes a unique contribution to the glory of God. That's community, a fellowship of little people who together make God visible in the world.

Lifting our lives to others happens every time we speak or act in ways that make our lives lives for others. When we are fully able to embrace our own lives, we discover that what we claim we also want to proclaim. A life well held is indeed a life for others. We stop wondering whether our life is better or worse than others and start seeing clearly that when we live our life for others we not only claim our individuality but also proclaim our unique place in the mosaic of the human family.

So often we are inclined to keep our lives hidden. Shame and guilt prevent us from letting others know what we are living. We think: "If my family and friends knew the dark cravings of my heart and my strange mental wanderings, they would push me away and exclude me from their company." But the opposite is true. When we dare to lift our cup and let our friends know what is in it, they will be encouraged to lift their cups and share with us their own anxiously hidden secrets. The greatest healing often takes place when we no longer feel isolated by our shame and guilt and discover that others often feel what we feel and think what we think and have the fears, apprehensions, and preoccupations we have.

Lifting our cup means sharing our life so we can celebrate it. When we truly believe we are called to lay down our lives for our friends, we must dare to take the risk to let others know what we are living. The important question is, "Do we have a circle of trustworthy friends where we feel safe enough to be intimately known and called to an always greater maturity?" Just as we lift up our glasses to people we trust and love, so we lift up the cup of our life to those from whom we do not want to have secrets and with whom we want to form community.

When we do want to drink our cup and drink it to the bottom, we need others who are willing to drink their cups with us. We need community, a community in which confession and celebration are always present together. We have to be willing to let others know us if we want them to celebrate life with us. When we lift our cups and say "to life," we should be talking about real lives, not only hard, painful, sorrowful lives, but also lives so full of joy that celebration becomes a spontaneous response.

CHAPTER FIVE

The Cup of Blessings

Lifting the cup is offering a blessing. The cup of sorrow and joy, when lifted for others "to life," becomes the cup of blessings.

I have a very lively memory connected with the cup of sorrow and joy becoming the cup of blessings. A few years ago, one of the handicapped members of the Daybreak community had to spend a few months in a mental hospital near Toronto for psychological evaluation. His name is Trevor. Trevor and I had become close friends over the years. He loved me and I loved him. Whenever he saw me coming, he ran up to me with a great radiant smile. Often he went into the fields and collected wildflowers for me. He always wanted to assist me in the celebrations of the Eucharist and had a fine sense for ceremony and ritual.

During the time Trevor was away from Daybreak, I decided to go see him. I called the hospital chaplain and asked him if I could visit my friend. He said I was welcome to come and wondered if it would be all right if he invited some of the ministers and priests in the area and some members of the hospital staff to have lunch with me. Without thinking much about the implications of this request, I said immediately, "Sure, that will be fine."

When I arrived at 11:00 A.M., a large group of clergy and hospital personnel was waiting for me, and they welcomed me warmly. I looked around for Trevor, but he wasn't there. So I said: "I came here to visit Trevor. Can you tell me where I can find him?" The hospital chaplain said: "You can be with him after lunch." I was stunned and said, "But didn't you invite him for lunch?" "No, no," he said, "that's impossible. Staff and patients cannot have lunch together. Moreover, we have reserved the Golden Room for this occasion, and no patient has ever been allowed in that room. It is for staff only." "Well," I said, "I will only have lunch with you all when

Trevor can be there too. Trevor and I are close friends. It is for him that I came, and I am sure he would love to join us for lunch." I noticed some mixed reactions to my words, but after some whispering I was told that I could bring Trevor with me to the Golden Room.

I found Trevor on the hospital grounds, as always, looking for flowers. When he saw me his face lit up, and he ran up to me as if we had never been apart and said: "Henri, here are some flowers for you." Together we went to the Golden Room. The table was beautifully set, and about twenty-five people had gathered around it. Trevor and I were the last to sit down.

After the opening prayer, Trevor walked to the side table where there were different drinks: wine, soft drinks, and juices. He said: "Henri, I want a Coke." I poured him a Coke, took a glass of wine for myself, and returned to the table.

People were making small talk. Many of the guests were strangers trying to get to know each other. The general atmosphere was quiet, somewhat solemn. I got quickly involved in a conversation with my right-hand neighbor and

70

didn't pay much attention to Trevor. But suddenly Trevor stood up, took his glass of Coke, lifted it, and said with a loud voice and a big smile: "Ladies and gentlemen . . . a toast!" Everyone dropped their conversation and turned to Trevor with puzzled and somewhat anxious faces. I could read their thoughts: "What in the heck is this patient going to do? Better be careful."

But Trevor had no worries. He looked at everybody and said: "Lift up your glasses." Everyone obeyed. And then, as if it were the most obvious thing to do, he started to sing: "When you're happy and you know it . . . lift your glass. When you're happy and you know it . . . lift your glass. When you're happy and you know it, when you're happy and you know it, when you're happy and you know it . . . lift your glass." As he sang, people's faces relaxed and started to smile. Soon a few joined Trevor in his song, and not long after everyone was standing, singing loudly under Trevor's direction.

Trevor's toast radically changed the mood in the Golden Room. He had brought these strangers together and made them feel at home.

His beautiful smile and his fearless joy had broken down the barriers between staff and patients and created a happy family of caring people. With his unique blessing, Trevor had set the tone for a joyful and fruitful meeting. The cup of sorrow and joy had become the cup of blessings.

Many people feel cursed—cursed by God with illnesses, losses, handicaps, and misfortunes. They believe their cup doesn't carry any blessings. It is the cup of God's wrath, the cup Jeremiah speaks of when he says:

> For Yahweh, the God of Israel said this to me, "Take this cup of the wine of wrath and make all the nations to whom I send you drink it; they will drink and reel and lose their wits, because of the sword I am sending among them. . . . You will say to them, 'Yahweh Sabaoth, the God of Israel, says this: Drink! Get drunk! Vomit! Fall, never to rise again, before the sword that I am sending among

you!' If they refuse to take the cup from your hand and drink, you will say to them, 'Yahweh Sabaoth says this: You must drink! Look, for a start, I am bringing disaster on the city that bears my name, so are you likely to go unpunished? You certainly will not go unpunished, for next I shall summon a sword against all the inhabitants of the land, Yahweh declares.'"

(Jeremiah 25:15–16, 27–29)

This is not a cup to lift "to life." It only brings misery. It is not surprising that no one wants to get close to the vengeful god that Jeremiah depicts. No blessing is found there. But when Jesus takes the cup on the evening before his death, it is not the cup of wrath but the cup of blessings. It is the cup of a new and everlasting covenant, the cup that unites us with God and with one another in a community of love. Paul writes to the people of Corinth: "I am talking to you as sensible people; weigh up for yourselves what I have to say. The blessing-cup, which we bless, is it not a sharing in the blood of Christ?" (1 Corinthians 10:15–16).

The immense suffering of humanity can easily be understood as a sign of God's wrath, as a punishment. It often was understood that way, and it often still is. The Psalmist says: "Yahweh is holding a cup filled with a heady blend of wine; he will pour it, they will drink it to the dregs, all the wicked on earth will drink it" (Psalm 75:8). And we, looking at the horrors that plague our world, are saying, "How can there be a loving God when all this is happening? It must be a cruel, spiteful God who allows human beings to suffer so much!"

Jesus, however, took upon himself all this suffering and lifted it up on the cross, not as a curse but as a blessing. Jesus made the cup of God's wrath into a cup of blessings. That's the mystery of the Eucharist. Jesus died for us so that we may live. He poured out his blood for us so that we may find new life. He gave himself away for us, so that we can live in community. He became for us food and drink so that we can be fed for everlasting life. That is what Jesus meant when he took the cup and said: "This cup is the new covenant in my blood poured out for you" (Luke 22:20). The Eucharist is that sacred mystery through which what we lived as a curse we now live as a blessing. Our suffering can no longer be a divine punishment. Jesus transformed it as the way to new life. His blood, and ours too, now can become martyr's blood — blood that witnesses to a new covenant, a new communion, a new community.

When we lift the cup of our life and share with one another our sufferings and joys in mutual vulnerability, the new covenant can become visible among us. The surprise of it all is that it is often the least among us who reveal to us that our cup is a cup of blessings.

Trevor did what nobody else could have done. He transformed a group of strangers into a community of love by his simple, unself-conscious blessing. He, a meek man, became the living Christ among us. The cup of blessings is the cup the meek have to offer to us.

CHAPTER SIX

To Life

We lift the cups of our lives to bring life to each other.

In the Daybreak community, celebration is an essential part of our life together. We celebrate birthdays and anniversaries, we celebrate those who arrive and those who depart, we celebrate birth and death, we celebrate commitments made and commitments renewed.

In our community there are many parties. Parties are usually happy events, during which we eat and drink, sing and dance, give speeches, talk and laugh a lot. But a celebration is something more than just than a party. A celebration is an occasion to lift up each other's lives—whether in a joyful or a sorrowful moment—and deepen our bonds with each other. To celebrate life is to raise up life, make it visible to each other, affirm it in its concreteness, and be grateful for it.

One very moving celebration I remember was that of Bill's *Life Story Book*. A *Life Story Book* is a collection of photographs, stories, and letters put together as a sort of biography. When Bill came to Daybreak as a sixteen-year-old, he brought few memories with him. He had had a very troublesome childhood and hardly any consistent experiences of love and friendship. His past was so broken, so painful, and so lonely that he had chosen to forget it. He was a man without a history.

But during twenty-five years at Daybreak, he gradually has become a different person. He has made friends. He has developed a close relationship with a family he can visit on weekends or holidays, joined a bowling club, learned woodworking, and traveled with me to places far and wide. Over the years he has created a life worth remembering. He even found the freedom and the courage to recall some of his painful childhood experiences and to reclaim his deceased parents as people who had given him life and love notwithstanding their limitations.

Now there was enough material for a *Life Story Book* because now there was a beautiful although painful story to tell. Many friends wrote letters to Bill telling him what they remembered about him. Others sent photographs or newspaper clippings about events he had been part of, and others just made drawings that expressed their love for him. After six months of work, the book was finally ready, and it was time to celebrate, not just the new book but Bill's life, which it symbolized.

Many came together for the occasion in the Dayspring Chapel. Bill held the book and lifted it up for all to see. It was a beautifully colored ring binder with many artistically decorated pages. Although it was Bill's book, it was the work of many people.

Then we blessed the book and Bill, who held it. I prayed that this book might help Bill let many people know what a beautiful man he is and what a good life he was living. I also prayed that Bill would remember all the moments of his life—his joys as well as his sorrows—with a grateful heart.

While I prayed tears started to flow from Bill's eyes. When I finished he threw his arms around me and cried loudly. His tears fell on my shoulder while everyone in the circle looked at us with a deep understanding of what was happening. Bill's life had been lifted up for all to see, and he had been able to say it was a life to be grateful for.

Now Bill takes his *Life Story Book* with him on his trips. He shows it to people as a man who believes his life is not something to be ashamed of. To the contrary, it is a gift for others.

The cup of sorrow and joy, when lifted for others to see and celebrate, becomes a cup to life. It is so easy for us to live truncated lives because of hard things that have happened in our past, which we prefer not to remember. Often the burdens of our past seem too heavy for us to carry alone. Shame and guilt make us hide part of ourselves and thus make us live half lives.

We truly need each other to claim all of our lives and to live them to the fullest. We need each other to move beyond our guilt and shame and to become grateful, not just for our successes and accomplishments but also for our failures and shortcomings. We need to be able to let our tears flow freely, tears of sorrow as well as tears of joy, tears that are as rain on dry ground. As we thus lift our lives for each other, we can truly say: "To life," because all we have lived now becomes the fertile soil for the future.

But lifting our cup to life is much more than saying good things about each other. It is much more than offering good wishes. It means that we take all we have ever lived and bring it to the present moment as a gift for others, a gift to celebrate.

Mostly we are willing to look back at our lives and say: "I am grateful for the *good* things that brought me to this place." But when we lift our cup to life, we must dare to say: "I am grateful for *all* that has happened to me and led me to this moment." This gratitude which embraces all of our past is what makes our life a true gift for others, because this gratitude erases bitterness, resentments, regret, and revenge as well as all jealousies and rivalries. It transforms our past into a fruitful gift for the future, and makes our life, all of it, into a life that gives life.

The enormous individualism of our society, in which so much emphasis is on "doing it yourself," prevents us from lifting our lives for each other. But each time we dare to step beyond our fear, to be vulnerable and lift our cup, our own and other people's lives will blossom in unexpected ways.

Then we too will find the strength to drink our cup and drink it to the bottom.

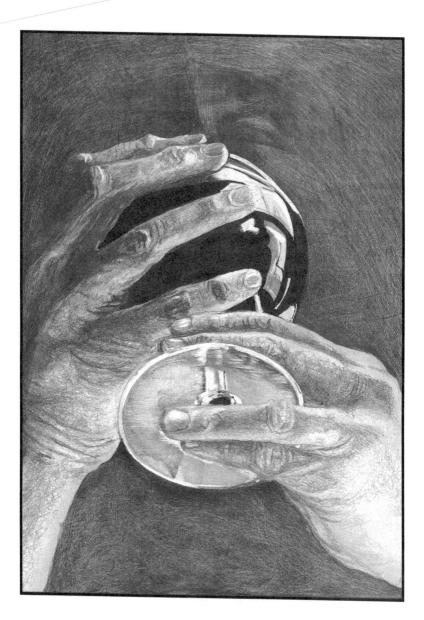

PART THREE

Drinking the Cup

CHAPTER SEVEN

Drinking

The cup that we hold and lift we must drink.

I have very vivid memories of my first year at the University of Nijmegen in Holland. I had just been ordained a priest, and Cardinal Alfrink had sent me to the Catholic university to work for a degree in psychology. But before the school year started, I had to undergo a long hazing process to be accepted into the student society and to become a member of a fraternity. Drinking beer was definitely one of the ways to get in! I wasn't used to drinking that much beer and had a hard time showing any prowess in this domain. But once I was finally admitted into the society and had made some friends in the fraternity, "having a drink together" became an expression for sharing, personal attention, good conversation, and the deepening of fellowship. "Let's have a beer!" "Can you join me for coffee?" "Let's meet for tea." "May I offer you a Heineken?" "What about another glass of wine?" "Come on, don't be shy, let me pour you another . . . you deserve it!" These and other similar ways of speaking created an atmosphere of companionship and conviviality.

In whatever country or culture we find ourselves, having a drink together is a sign of friendship, intimacy, and peace. Being thirsty is often not the main reason to drink. We drink to "break the ice," to enter into a conversation, to show good intention, to express friendship and goodwill, to set the stage for a romantic moment, to be open, vulnerable, accessible. It is no surprise that people who are angry at us, or who come to accuse us or harass us, won't accept a drink from us. They would rather say: "I will come straight to the point of my being here." Refusing a drink is avoiding intimacy.

At worst, drinking together is saying, "We trust each other enough that we don't want to poison each other." At best, it is saying, "I want to get close to you and celebrate life with you." It breaks through the boundaries that separate us

and invites us to recognize our shared humanity. Thus, drinking together can be a true spiritual event, affirming our unity as children of one
God.

The world is full of places to drink: bars,
pubs, coffee and tea rooms. Even when we go
out to eat, the waiter's first question is always
"Can I offer you something to drink?" That is
also one of the first questions we ask our guests
when they enter our home.

It seems that most of our drinking takes
place in a context in which we feel, at least for a
moment, at home with ourselves and safe with
others. Drinking a cup of coffee to interrupt
work for a moment, stopping for tea in the after-
noon, having a "quick drink" before dinner, taking a glass of wine before going to bed—all these
are moments to say to ourselves or others: "It is
good to be alive in the midst of all that is going
on, and I want to be reminded of that."

Drinking the cup of life makes our own
everything we are living. It is saying, "This is
my life," but also "I want this to be my life."
Drinking the cup of life is fully appropriating

and internalizing our own unique existence, with all its sorrows and joys.

It is not easy to do this. For a long time we might not feel capable of accepting our own life; we might keep fighting for a better or at least a different life. Often a deep protest against our "fate" rises in us. We didn't choose our country, our parents, the color of our skin, our sexual orientation. We didn't even choose our character, intelligence, physical appearance, or mannerisms. Sometimes we want to do every possible thing to change the circumstances of our life. We wish we were in another body, lived in another time, or had another mind! A cry can come out of our depths: "Why do I have to be this person? I didn't ask for it, and I don't want it."

But as we gradually come to befriend our own reality, to look with compassion at our own sorrows and joys, and as we are able to discover the unique potential of our way of being in the world, we can move beyond our protest, put the cup of our life to our lips and drink it, slowly, carefully, but fully.

Often when we wish to comfort people, we say: "Well, it is sad this has happened to you, but try to make the best of it." But "making the best of it" is not what drinking the cup is about. Drinking our cup is not simply adapting ourselves to a bad situation and trying to use it as well as we can. Drinking our cup is a hopeful, courageous, and self-confident way of living. It is standing in the world with head erect, solidly rooted in the knowledge of who we are, facing the reality that surrounds us and responding to it from our hearts.

The great figures in history looked deeply into their cups and drank from them without fear. Whether they were famous or not, they knew that the life which was given to them was given to live to its fullness in the presence of God and God's people, and thus bear much fruit. They needed to make it bear fruit. Jesus, the carpenter's son from Nazareth—"Can anything good come from Nazareth?" people asked (John 1:46)—drank his cup to the bitter end. All his disciples did too, different as they may have been.

Spiritual greatness has nothing to do with being greater than others. It has everything to do with being as great as each of us can be. True sanctity is precisely drinking our own cup and trusting that by thus fully claiming our own, irreplaceable journey, we can become a source of hope for many. Vincent van Gogh, miserable and brokenhearted as he was, believed without question in his vocation to paint, and he went as far as he could with what little he had. This is true for Francis of Assisi, Dorothy Day of New York, and Oscar Romero of San Salvador. Small people, but great in drinking their cups to the full.

How then can we, in the midst of our ordinary daily lives, drink our cup, the cup of sorrow and the cup of joy? How can we fully appropriate what is given to us? Somehow we know that when we do not drink our cup and thus avoid the sorrow as well as the joy of living, our lives become inauthentic, insincere, superficial, and boring. We become puppets moved up and down, left and right by the puppeteers of this world. We become objects, yes, victims of other people's interests and desires. But we don't have to be victims. We can choose to drink the cup of our life with the deep conviction that by drinking it we will find our true freedom. Thus, we will discover that the cup of sorrow and joy we are drinking is the cup of salvation.

CHAPTER EIGHT

The Cup of Salvation

Gordie Henry, who has Down's syndrome, is one of the core members of the Daybreak community. Once he said to me, "What is good about our life is that you make so many friends. What is hard about our life is that so many friends leave." With this simple observation Gordie touched the place where joy and sorrow are embracing each other. As a longtime member of Daybreak, Gordie has had many assistants come to live with him. They came from various countries, sometimes for a summer, sometimes for a year, sometimes for many years. They all loved Gordie very much, and Gordie came to love them. Strong attachments and deep bonds of friendship developed.

But sooner or later, the assistants had to leave. Some got married, some returned to school, some lost their work permits, some looked for a new direction in life, and some discovered that community life wasn't for them. Gordie, however, stayed, and felt the intense pain of the many separations.

One day, Jean Vanier, the founder of l'Arche, came to visit Daybreak. He gathered the whole community around him and said, "What questions would you most like to ask me?" Thelus, one of the core members who had lived at Daybreak as long as Gordie, raised her hand and said: "Why are people leaving all the time?" Jean understood this question was not just Thelus' question but also Gordie's question and the question of all long-term Daybreak members.

He gently moved closer to her and said: "You know, Thelus, that *is* the most important question you can ask. Because you and many others want to make Daybreak your home, where you can feel well loved and well protected. What then does it mean when so often someone you love, and who loves you, leaves your home, sometimes for good? Why then do you have to suffer the pain of so many departures? It may feel as if people do not really love you! Because if they love you, why would they leave you?"

As he was speaking, everyone looked at him very attentively. They knew this man truly understood their pain and sincerely cared for them. They wanted to hear what he had to say. With great gentleness and compassion, Jean looked at everyone who was listening and said: "You know, your joy and your pain give you a mission. Those who came to live with you, from whom you received much and to whom you gave much, aren't just leaving you. You are sending them back to their schools, their homes, and their families, to bring some of the love they have lived with you. It's hard. It's painful to let them go. But when you realize that this is a mission, you will be able to send your friends to continue their journeys without losing the joy they brought you."

These simple words entered deep into our hearts because they made us look differently at what had seemed such a harsh tearing apart. The cup of joy and sorrow had become the cup of salvation.

Drinking the cup of sorrow and joy is only possible when it bring us health, strength, freedom, hope, courage—new life. Nobody will drink the cup of life when it makes us sick and miserable. We can only drink it when it is a cup of salvation.

This is beautifully expressed in Psalm 116:

The Lord is merciful and upright,
our God is tenderness. . . .
My trust does not fail even when
I say,
"I am completely wretched."
In my terror I said,
"No human being can be relied
on."
What return can I make to the
Lord
for his generosity to me?
I shall take up the cup of
salvation
and call on the name of the Lord.
(Psalm 116:5, 10-13. The word "Yahweh" is
replaced by "Lord.")

Here the mystery of drinking the cup becomes clear. The coming and leaving of friends, the experiences of love and betrayal, of care and indifference, of generosity and stinginess can become the way to true human freedom. Yes, people who love us also disappoint us, moments of great satisfaction also reveal unfulfilled needs, being home also shows us our homelessness. But all of these tensions can create in us that deep, deep yearning for full freedom that is beyond any of the structures of our world.

Indeed, there is a mission emerging out of a life that is never pure sorrow or pure joy, a mission that makes us move far beyond our human limitations and reach out to total freedom, complete redemption, ultimate salvation.

Jesus drank the cup of his life. He experienced praise, adulation, admiration, and immense popularity. He also experienced rejection, ridicule, and mass hatred. At one moment people shouted "Hosanna"; a moment later they cried: "Crucify him." Jesus took it all in, not as a hero adored and then vilified, but as the one who had come to fulfill a mission and who kept his focus on that mission whatever the responses were. Jesus knew deep within himself that he had to drink the cup to accomplish the work his

Abba—his dear Father—had given him. He knew that drinking the cup would bring him freedom, glory, and wholeness. He knew that drinking the cup would lead him beyond the entrapment of this world to complete liberation, beyond the agony of death to the splendor of the resurrection. This knowing had little to do with understanding or comprehending. It was a knowledge of a heart shaped in the garden of eternal love.

Thus the cup which Jesus was willing to drink, and which he drank until it was completely empty, became the cup of salvation. In the garden of Gethsemane, the garden of fear, Jesus' heart cried out with the psalmist: "No human being can be relied on. . . . I shall take up the cup of salvation and call on the name of the Lord." Drinking the cup of salvation means emptying the cup of sorrow and joy so that God can fill it with pure life.

"Salvation" is about being saved. But from what do we need to be saved? The traditional answer—and the good one—is sin and death. We are entrapped by sin and death as in a hunter's snare.

When we think for a moment of various addictions—alcohol, drug, food, gambling, sex—we get some idea of that entrapment.

In addition there are our many compulsions. We can feel compelled to act, speak, and even think in one way without being able to choose any other way. When people say: "Be sure you clean the room before you leave it, otherwise he gets raving mad!" or "Whatever she does, she first needs to wash her hands," we know that we are dealing with compulsive people.

Finally, all of us have our obsessions. An idea, a plan, a hobby can obsess us to such a degree that we become its slave.

These addictions, compulsions, and obsessions reveal our entrapments. They show our sinfulness because they take away our freedom as children of God and thus enslave us in a cramped, shrunken world. Sin makes us want to create our own lives according to our desires and wishes, ignoring the cup that is given to us. Sin makes us self-indulgent. St. Paul says: "When self-indulgence is at work the results are obvious: sexual vice, impurity, and sensuality, the worship of false gods and sorcery; antagonisms and rivalry, jealousy, bad temper and quarrels, disagreements, factions and malice, drunkenness, orgies and all such things" (Galatians 5:18-21).

Death too entraps us. Death is surrounding us on all sides: the threat of nuclear death; the reality of death caused by the many international, national, and ethnic conflicts; the death resulting from starvation and neglect; the death through abortion and euthanasia; and the death coming from the countless diseases that plague humanity, especially AIDS and cancer. Sooner or later the inevitability of our own deaths will catch up with us. In whatever direction we run, death is there, never leaving us completely alone. Not a day passes in which we are not worried about the health of a family member, a friend, or ourselves. Not a day passes that we aren't reminded of those snares of death.

Sin and death entrap us. Drinking the cup, as Jesus did, is the way out of that trap. It is the way to salvation. It is a hard way, a painful way, a way we want to avoid at all costs. Often it even seems an impossible way. Still, unless we are willing to drink our cup, real freedom will elude us. This is not only the freedom that comes after we have completely emptied our cup—that is, after we have died. No, this freedom comes to us every time we drink from the cup of life, whether a little or much.

Salvation is not only a goal for the afterlife. Salvation is a reality of every day that we can taste here and now. When I sit down with Adam and help him eat, chat with Bill about our next trip, have coffee with Susanne and breakfast with David, when I embrace Michael, kiss Patsy, or pray with Gordie, salvation is right there. And when we sit together around the low altar table and I offer to all present the glass cup filled with wine, I can announce with great certainty: "This is the cup of salvation."

CHAPTER NINE

To the Bottom

*The question now is: How do we
drink the cup of salvation?*

We have to drink our cup slowly, tasting every mouthful—all the way to the bottom! Living a complete life is drinking our cup until it is empty, trusting that God will fill it with everlasting life.

It is important, however, to be very specific when we deal with the question "How do we drink our cup?" We need some very concrete disciplines to help us fully appropriate and internalize our joys and sorrows and find in them our unique way to spiritual freedom. I would like to explore how three disciplines—the discipline of silence, the discipline of the word, and the discipline of action—can help us drink our cup of salvation.

The first way to drink our cup is in silence.

This might come as a surprise, since being silent seems like doing nothing, but it is precisely in silence that we confront our true selves. The sorrows of our lives often overwhelm us to such a degree that we will do everything not to face them. Radio, television, newspapers, books, films, but also hard work and a busy social life all can be ways to run away from ourselves and turn life into a long entertainment.

The word *entertainment* is important here. It means literally "to keep (*tain* from the Latin *tenere*) someone in between (*enter*)." Entertainment is everything that gets and keeps our mind away from things that are hard to face. Entertainment keeps us distracted, excited, or in suspense. Entertainment is often good for us. It gives us an evening or a day off from our worries and fears. But when we start living life as entertainment, we lose touch with our souls and become little more than spectators in a lifelong show. Even very useful and relevant work can become a way of forgetting who we really are. It is no surprise that for many people retirement is a fearful prospect. Who are we when there is nothing to keep us busy?

Silence is the discipline that helps us to go beyond the entertainment quality of our lives. There we can let our sorrows and joys emerge from their hidden place and look us in the face, saying: "Don't be afraid; you can look at your own journey, its dark and light sides, and discover your way to freedom." We may find silence in nature, in our own houses, in a church or meditation hall. But wherever we find it, we should cherish it. Because it is in silence that we can truly acknowledge who we are and gradually claim ourselves as a gift from God.

At first silence might only frighten us. In silence we start hearing the voices of darkness: our jealousy and anger, our resentment and desire for revenge, our lust and greed, and our pain over losses, abuses, and rejections. These voices are often noisy and boisterous. They may even deafen us. Our most spontaneous reaction is to run away from them and return to our entertainment.

But if we have the discipline to stay put and not let these dark voices intimidate us, they will gradually lose their strength and recede into the background, creating space for the softer, gentler voices of the light.

These voices speak of peace, kindness, gentleness, goodness, joy, hope, forgiveness, and, most of all, love. They might at first seem small and insignificant, and we may have a hard time trusting them. However, they are very persistent and they will grow stronger if we keep listening. They come from a very deep place and from very far. They have been speaking to us since before we were born, and they reveal to us that there is no darkness in the One who sent us into the world, only light. They are part of God's voice calling us from all eternity: "My beloved child, my favorite one, my joy."

The enormous powers of our world keep drowning out these gentle voices. Still, they are the voices of truth. They are like the voice that Elijah heard on Mount Horeb. There God passed him not in a hurricane, an earthquake, or a fire but in "a light murmuring sound" (1 Kings

19:11–13). This sound takes away our fear and makes us realize that we can face reality, especially our own reality. Being in silence is the first way we learn to drink our cup.

The second way to drink our cup is with the word. It is not enough to claim our sorrow and joy in silence. We also must claim them in a trusted circle of friends. To do so we need to speak about what is in our cup. As long as we live our deepest truth in secret, isolated from a community of love, its burden is too heavy to carry. The fear of being known can make us split off our true inner selves from our public selves and make us despise ourselves even when we are acclaimed and praised by many.

To know ourselves truly and acknowledge fully our own unique journey, we need to be known and acknowledged by others for who we are. We cannot live a spiritual life in secrecy. We cannot find our way to true freedom in isolation. Silence without speaking is as dangerous as solitude without community. They belong together.

Speaking about our cup and what it holds is not easy. It requires a true discipline because, just as we want to run from silence in order to avoid self-confrontation, we want to run from speaking about our inner life in order to avoid confrontation with others.

I am not suggesting that everyone we know or meet should hear about what is in our cup. To the contrary, it would be tactless, unwise, and even dangerous to expose our innermost being to people who cannot offer us safety and trust. That does not create community; it only causes mutual embarrassment and deepens our shame and guilt. But I do suggest that we need loving and caring friends with whom we can speak from the depth of our heart. Such friends can take away the paralysis that secrecy creates. They can offer us a safe and sacred place, where we can express our deepest sorrows and joys, and they can confront us in love, challenging us to a greater spiritual maturity. We might object by saying: "I do not have such trustworthy friends, and I wouldn't know how to find them." But this objection comes from our fear of drinking the cup that Jesus asks us to drink.

When we are fully committed to the spiritual adventure of drinking our cup to the bottom, we will soon discover that people who are on the same journey will offer themselves to us for encouragement and friendship and love. It has been my own most blessed experience that God sends wonderful friends to those who make God their sole concern. This is the mysterious paradox Jesus speaks about when he says that when we leave those who are close to us, for his sake and the sake of the Gospel, we will receive a hundred times more in human support (see Mark 10:29-30).

When we dare to speak from the depth of our heart to the friends God gives us, we will gradually find new freedom within us and new courage to live our own sorrows and joys to the full. When we truly believe that we have nothing to hide from God, we need to have people around us who represent God for us and to whom we can reveal ourselves with complete trust.

Nothing will give us so much strength as being fully known and fully loved by fellow human beings in the Name of God. That gives us the courage to drink our cup to the bottom, knowing it is the cup of our salvation. It will allow us not only to live well but to die well. When we are surrounded by loving friends, death becomes a gateway to the full communion of saints.

The third way to drink our cup is in action.

Action, just as silence and the word, can help us to claim and celebrate our true self. But here again we need discipline, because the world in which we live says: "Do this, do that, go here, go there, meet him, meet her." Busyness has become a sign of importance. Having much to do, many places to go, and countless people to meet gives us status and even fame. However, being busy can lead us away from our true vocation and prevent us from drinking our cup.

It is not easy to distinguish between doing what we are called to do and doing what we want to do. Our many wants can easily distract us from our true action. True action leads us to the fulfillment of our vocation. Whether we work in an office, travel the world, write books or make films, care for the poor, offer leadership, or fulfill unspectacular tasks, the question is not "What do I most want?" but "What is my vocation?" The most prestigious position in society can be an expression of obedience to our call as well as a sign of our refusal to hear that call, and the least prestigious position, too, can be a response to our vocation as well as a way to avoid it.

Drinking our cup involves carefully choosing those actions which lead us closer to complete emptying of it, so that at the end of our lives we can say with Jesus: "It is fulfilled" (John 19:30). That indeed, is the paradox: We fulfill life by emptying it. In Jesus' own words: "Anyone who loses his life for my sake will find it" (Matthew 10:39).

When we are committed to do God's will and not our own we soon discover that much of what we do doesn't need to be done by us. What we are called to do are actions that bring us true joy and peace. Just as leaving friends for the sake of the Gospel will bring us friends, so too will letting go of actions not in accord with our call.

Actions that lead to overwork, exhaustion, and burnout can't praise and glorify God. What

God calls us to do we *can* do and do *well*. When we listen in silence to God's voice and speak with our friends in trust we will know what we are called to do and we will do it with a grateful heart.

Silence, speaking, and acting are three disciplines to help us to drink our cup. They are disciplines because we do not practice them spontaneously. In a world that encourages us to avoid the real life issues, these disciplines ask for concentrated effort. But if we keep choosing silence, a circle of trusting friends to speak with, and actions that flow from our call, we are in fact drinking our cup, bit by bit, to the bottom. The sorrows of our lives will no longer paralyze us, nor will our joys make us lose perspective. The disciplines of silence, word, and action focus our eyes on the road we are traveling and help us to move forward, step by step, to our goal. We will encounter great obstacles and splendid views, long, dry deserts and also freshwater lakes surrounded by shadow-rich trees. We will have to fight against those who try to attack and rob us. We also will make wonderful friends. We will often wonder if we will ever make it, but one day we will see coming to us the One who has been waiting for us from all eternity to welcome us home.

Yes, we can drink our cup of life to the bottom, and as we drink it we will realize that the One who has called us "the Beloved," even before we were born, is filling it with everlasting life.

The Answer

I have looked at many cups: golden, silver, bronze, and glass cups, splendidly decorated and very simple cups, elegantly shaped and very plain cups. Whatever their material, form, or value, they all speak about drinking. Drinking, like eating, is one of the most universal of human acts. We drink to stay alive, or we drink ourselves to death. When people say: "He drinks a lot," we think of alcoholism and family trouble. But when they say: "I wish you could come over to have a drink with us," we think about hospitality, celebration, friendship, and intimacy.

It is no surprise that the cup is such a universal symbol. It embodies much that goes on in our lives.

Many cups speak of victory; soccer cups, football cups, and tennis cups are eagerly desired trophies. Pictures of captains holding a victory cup while being carried triumphantly on the shoulders of their teams are imprinted in our memories as reminders of our excitement at winning moments. These cups speak of success, bravery, heroism, fame, popularity, and great power.

Many cups also speak of death. Joseph's silver cup, found in Benjamin's sack, spelled doom. The cups of Isaiah and Jeremiah are the cups of God's wrath and destruction. Socrates' cup was a poisonous one given to him for his execution.

The cup that Jesus speaks about is neither a symbol of victory nor a symbol of death. It is a symbol of life, filled with sorrows and joys that we can hold, lift, and drink as a blessing and a way to salvation. "Can you drink the cup that I am going to drink?" Jesus asks us. It is the question that will have a different meaning every day of our lives. Can we embrace fully the sorrows and joys that come to us day after day? At one moment it might seem so easy to drink the cup, and we give a quick yes to Jesus' question. Shortly afterwards everything might look and feel quite different, and our whole being might cry out, "No, never!" We have to let the yes and the no both speak in us so that we can come to know ever more deeply the enormous challenge of Jesus' question.

John and James had not the faintest idea of what they were saying when they said yes. They hardly understood who Jesus was. They didn't think about him as a leader who would be betrayed, tortured, and killed on a cross. Nor did they dream about their own lives as marked by tiresome travels and harsh persecutions, and consumed by contemplation or martyrdom. Their first easy yes had to be followed by many hard yeses until their cups were completely empty.

And what is the reward of it all? John and James' mother wanted a concrete reward: "Promise that these two sons of mine may sit one at your right hand and the other at your left in your kingdom" (Matthew 20:21). She and they had little doubt about what they wanted. They wanted power, influence, success, and wealth. They were preparing themselves for a significant role when the Roman occupiers would be thrown out and Jesus would be king and have his own cabinet of ministers.

They wanted to be his right- and left-hand men in the new political order.

Still, notwithstanding all their misperceptions, they had been deeply touched by this man Jesus. In his presence they had experienced something radically new, something that went beyond anything they had ever imagined. It had to do with inner freedom, love, care, hope, and, most of all, with God. Yes, they wanted power and influence, but beyond that they wanted to stay close to Jesus at all costs. As their journey continued, they gradually discovered what they had said yes to. They heard about being a servant instead of a master, about seeking the last place instead of the first, about giving up their lives instead of controlling other people's lives. Each time they had to make a choice again. Did they want to stay with Jesus or leave? Did they want to follow the way of Jesus or look for someone else who could give them the power they desired?

Later Jesus challenged them directly: "What about you, do you want to go away?" Peter responded: "Lord, to whom shall we go? You have the message of eternal life, and we believe; we have come to know that you are the Holy One of God" (John 6:67-69). He and his friends had started to glimpse the Kingdom Jesus had been talking about. But again there was that question: "Can you drink the cup?" They said yes over and over. And what about the seats in the Kingdom? They might not be the kinds of seats they expected, but could they still be closer to Jesus than the other followers?

Jesus' answer is as radical as his question: ". . . as for seats at my right hand and my left, these are not mine to grant; they belong to those to whom they have been allotted by my Father" (Matthew 20:23). Drinking the cup is not a heroic act with a nice reward! It is not part of a tit-for-tat agreement. Drinking the cup is an act of selfless love, an act of immense trust, an act of surrender to a God who will give what we need when we need it.

Jesus' inviting us to drink the cup without offering the reward we expect is the great challenge of the spiritual life. It breaks through all human calculations and expectations. It defies all our wishes to be sure in advance. It turns our hope for a predictable future upside down and pulls down our self-invented safety devices. It asks for the most radical trust in God, the same trust that made Jesus drink the cup to the bottom.

Drinking the cup that Jesus drank is living a life in and with the spirit of Jesus, which is the spirit of unconditional love. The intimacy between Jesus and Abba, his Father, is an intimacy of complete trust, in which there are no power games, no mutually agreed upon promises, no advance guarantees. It is only love—pure, unrestrained, and unlimited love. Completely open, completely free. That intimacy gave Jesus the strength to drink his cup. That same intimacy Jesus wants to give us so that we can drink ours. That intimacy has a Name, a Divine Name. It is called Holy Spirit. Living a spiritual life is living a life in which the Holy Spirit will guide us and give us the strength and courage to keep saying *yes* to the great question.

One Cup, One Body

*On July 21, 1997, it will be forty years since
Cardinal Bernard Alfrink ordained me to the
priesthood and my uncle Anton gave me his
golden chalice.*

The next morning I celebrated my first
Mass in the sisters' chapel of the seminary. I
stood in front of the altar, with my back to the
sisters who had been so kind to me during my
six years of philosophical and theological stud-
ies, and slowly read all the Latin readings and
prayers. During the offertory I carefully held
the chalice. After the consecration I lifted it high
above my head so that the sisters could see it.
And during communion, after having taken and
given the consecrated bread, I drank from it as
the only one allowed to do so at that time.

It was an intimate and mystical experience.
The presence of Jesus was more real for me than

the presence of any friend could possibly be. Afterwards I knelt for a long time and was overwhelmed by the grace of my priesthood.

During the nearly forty years that have followed, I have celebrated the Eucharist every day with very few exceptions, and I can hardly conceive of my life without that consistent experience of intimate communion with Jesus. Still, many things have changed. Today I sit behind a low table in a circle of handicapped men and women. All of us read and pray in English. When the gifts of bread and wine are brought to the table, the wine is poured into large glass cups, held by me and the Eucharistic ministers. During the Eucharistic prayer the bread and the cups are lifted up so that everyone can see the consecrated gifts and experience that Christ is truly among us. Then the body and blood of Christ are offered as food and drink to everyone. And when we offer the cup to each other, we look each other in the eye and say: "The Blood of Christ."

This daily event has deepened our life together over the years and made us more conscious that what we live every day, our sorrows and joys, is an integral part of the great mystery of Christ's death and resurrection. This simple, nearly hidden celebration in the basement of our small house of prayer makes it possible to live our day not just as a random series of events, meetings, and encounters, but as the day the Lord has made to make his presence known to us.

So much has changed! So much has remained the same! Forty years ago, I couldn't have imagined being a priest in the way I am now. Still, it is the continuous participation in the compassionate priesthood of Jesus that makes these forty years look like one long, beautiful Eucharist, one glorious act of petition, praise, and thanksgiving.

The golden chalice became a glass cup, but what it holds has remained the same. It is the life of Christ and our life, blended together into one life. As we drink the cup, we drink the cup that Jesus drank, but we also drink *our* cup. That is the great mystery of the Eucharist. The cup of Jesus, filled with his life, poured out for us and all people, and our cup, filled with our own blood, have become one cup. Together when we drink that cup as Jesus drank it we are transformed into the one body of the living Christ, always dying and always rising for the salvation of the world.

 **Henri J.M. Nouwen** is one of the most popular spiritual writers of our time. He wrote more than forty books, among them the bestsellers *With Open Hands* and *Out of Solitude.* He taught at Yale University, Harvard University, and the University of Notre Dame. From 1986 until his death in 1996, he taught and ministered to physically and mentally challenged men and women as a member of the L'Arche Daybreak community in Toronto, Canada. Learn more about Nouwen's life and works at www.henrinouwen.org.

Ron Hansen is a highly regarded novelist and essayist. Among his many successful novels are National Book Award finalist *Atticus* and *The Assassination of Jesse James by the Coward Robert Ford,* which has been adapted into a major motion picture. Such works as *Atticus*, his novel *Mariette in Ecstasy*, and his collection of essays *A Stay Against Confusion* led the Catholic journal *America* to declare that he "join[ed] company with Bernanos and Greene as an explorer of the Catholic sensibility." He is currently the Gerard Manley Hopkins SJ Professor of the Arts and Humanities at Santa Clara University.

More from Henri J.M. Nouwen

Eternal Seasons
A Spiritual Journey through the Church's Year
Edited by Michael Ford
ISBN: 9781594711473
256 pages / $12.95

Can You Drink the Cup?
Foreword by Ron Hansen
ISBN: 9781594710995
128 pages / $10.95

Behold the Beauty
Praying with Icons
Foreword by Robert Lentz
ISBN: 9781594711367
128 pages / $14.95

With Open Hands
Foreword by Sue Monk Kidd
ISBN: 9781594710643
128 pages / $9.95

Dance of Life
Weaving Sorrows and Blessings into One Joyful Step
Edited by Michael Ford
ISBN: 9781594710872
224 pages / $12.95

Out of Solitude
Three Meditations on the Christian Life
Foreword by Thomas Moore
ISBN: 9780877934950
64 pages / $7.95

Heart Speaks to Heart
Three Gospel Meditations on Jesus
ISBN: 9781594711169
64 pages / $7.95

A Restless Soul
Meditations from the Road
Edited by Michael Ford
ISBN: 9781594711633
160 pages / $11.95